D1530761

ALL MOROCCO

Text, photographs, design, lay-out and printing
entirely created by the technical department of
EDITORIAL ESCUDO DE ORO, S.A.

Rights of total or partial reproduction
and translation reserved.

Copyright of this edition for photographs and text:
© EDITORIAL ESCUDO DE ORO, S.A.

Distributed in Morocco: **TOP-PHOTO**
19. RUE HAY MASJID AL MOUHAMMADI HABBOUS.
CASABLANCA. MAROC
Tel. 30 62 58

Editorial Escudo de Oro, S.A.

The fantasia *or «gunpowder race».*

His Majesty King Hassan II. ▷

THE LONG AND BRILLIANT HISTORY OF MOROCCO

Situated at the western end of North Africa, also known as Africa Minor, Berbery, or Maghreb, the Kingdom of Morocco has a coastline that stretches from the Mediterranean to the Atlantic: a natural frontier. The Mediterranean coast is rugged, but the Atlantic side is much less so and has many fine beaches. A large fertile plain abounding in valleys and hills stretches between the Atlantic and the mountains. The Atlas Mountains –the peak at Toubkal reaches a height of 4,165 metres– are the spinal column of western Morocco, and the Rif mountains encircle the Mediterranean area.

Man's presence in this country dates from prehistoric times, as is shown by the discovery of fossilized human skeletons near Rabat, Casablanca and other cities, dating from the earlier and mid-paleolithic age and belonging to a human race with the same characteristics as Neanderthal man. It would appear that Morocco was inhabited during the later Palaeolithic age by a race very similar to *homo sapiens.* During the Neolithic age Phoenicians and Carthaginians reached northern Africa and Morocco entered history as a country.

After the arrival of the Berbers, Morocco was occupied by the Romans, Vandals and Byzantines. But the real history of Morocco began with the Arab conquest and the establishment of Islam at the end of the 3th century by Sherif Moulay Idris, great-grandson of Ali, son-in-law of Mohammed. It was Idris II, the posthumous son of Moulay Idris, who founded the first kingdom of Morocco.

Later on the Berber kingdoms of Berghouata, in what is now Chaouïa, and Sijilmassa in the region

Two views of the Venus Mosaic in the ruins of Volubilis.

of the oases, and the Arab kingdom of the Idrisids were created. When Idris II died at the beginning of the 9th century Berber kingdoms were again established in Morocco.

There was later a second Arab invasion, and in the 10th century the Almoravides founded a great empire in what is now Morocco. In the 12th century, the Almohade Ibn Toumert founded a new dynasty. His successor, Abd al Mumin, conquered the Moroccan Atlas and the main cities of Algeria, Tunisia and Andalusia. His son and grandson expanded the empire further, but the whole Almohade empire fell in the 13th century. Then came the Marinids and the Saadis, whose respective dynasties helped to establish Morocco's artistic and cultural heritage. In the middle of the 17th century, the Alawis replaced the Saadis and founded a dynasty, established by Moulay Ismaïl in Meknes, which had the honour of founding modern Morocco. Its independence was recognized by Mohammed V, rejecting the protectorates imposed by France and Spain. His son, His Majesty Hassan II, when he reintegrated the territory of the Sahara to his kingdom in 1975, consolidated the independence of the country.

RABAT

Capital of the kingdom of Morocco and seat of its government, Rabat is situated at the mouth of the river Bu Regreg, opposite the city of Sale. From the Hassan tower, dominating the ruins of the old mosque of which it was the minaret, there is a fine panoramic view with Rabat in the foreground, the estuary of the Bu Regreg, Salé, Chellah –the Roman *Sala Colonia*– and, on the horizon, the leafy wood of Mamora. Rabat consists of two clearly delineated areas: the medina, picturesque and full of vitality, and the new city with its modern urban development.

Rabat is a very old city and was among the resorts of *Tingitania.* The historian Ptolemy named it *Sale.* Apparently it acquired the status of a Roman municipality in the time of Trajan. Its present name, however, dates from the 8th century when Salih, the Berber chief of the Berghouta tribe, became a heresiarch of Islam and to defend himself from the orthodox built a *ribat,* which is a sort of fortified monastery. Towards the middle of the 12th century, the Almohades attacked the Berghouata, and a century later the Marinids replaced the Almohads.

Rabat was the place of many brilliant historical events during numerous centuries; and after being the seat of the Residency General during the French Protectorate, it became the administrative capital

The Bâb el-Had gate, Rabat.

Overall view of the Ahl Fass Royal Mosque and the Royal Palace.

A fine view of the Essounna Mosque.

of the kingdom when independence was granted to Morocco under Mohammed V.

At the present time Rabat has the attractive appearance of a warm, welcoming city, rationally urbanized. Although it is the administrative capital of Morocco, it still preserves the charm of a former provincial capital. The typically Moroccan buildings are characterized by the elegant style that the sovereigns of the reigning dynasty have lent to their architecture. Rabat is a city full of trees and flowers, with delightful gardens in agreeable contrast with the city buildings. A walk through the Belvedere Garden, the Oudaïa Garden, the Triangle Garden or the Experimental Garden is a real pleasure.

The most outstanding streets in Rabat are the Avenue Mohammed V, the busiest in the entire city, the Boulevar Hassan II, Rue Souq es Sebat, Place Souq el Ghezel and Rue Jamaa, the largest street in the attractive Kasba of the Oudaïa dynasty. The whole city is filled with surprises for the tourist's eye.

Besides the Hassan tower –the minaret of a Roman/Byzantine style mosque considered to be one of the greatest temples of Islam–, whose elegant silhouette reminds one of the Koutoubia in Marrakesh and the Giralda in Seville, the following monuments are of prime importance both historically and artistically: the royal palace, the Chellah, the city walls, the gateway of the Kasba of the Oudaïa dynasty, the Bab Er Rouah gate, the 14th-century Marinid fountain, the Great Mosque, the small Guazzarin Mosque and Mohammed V's mausoleum.

The Royal Palace was built during the second half of the 19th century on a site formerly occupied by the Palace of Sidi Mohammed ben Abdallah. Its most impressive feature is the majestic gateway in yellow stone. The large, sumptuous chambers have been restored and extensively decorated in recent years.

The gate of the Royal Palace.

The Chellah Gate

*Panoramic view
of Rabat.* ▷

*The ruins of Chellah,
and the mosque.*

The walls of the Udaya
fortress.

Overall view of the
Udaya gardens.

The Chellah is situated at the entrance to Rabat. This is a former Roman city of great architectural value, considered to be «the most romantic spot in Morocco».

Mohammed V's mausoleum is located on the esplanade of the Hassan mosque. The monarch's tomb is in a vast room with artistically decorated marble walls with a fine cedar-wood dome encrusted with gold leaf.

There are several extremely interesting museums in Rabat. In the Archaeological Museum there are works of incalculable value, the most outstanding of which are objects from the principal archaeological sites in the country, the geometrical mosaic from Volubilis that sums up the ancient history of Morocco, a large royal statue in white marble, jewels, cameos, and other interesting pieces.

The Museum of Moroccan Arts, the Scientific Institute and the Museum of Earth Sciences all have noteworthy collections.

There are many beaches in the environs of Rabat, among them those known as Little Smugglers, Temara, Golden Valley, Krick Rock, Golden Sands, Skhirat and Oued Ykem.

Another big tourist attraction of the Moroccan capital is its proximity to Salé, Rabat's twin city, surrounded by an exceptionally beautiful landscape and featuring many interesting monuments.

A traditional Moroccan room in the Hotel Tour Hassan.

The Hassan Tower.

Mausoleum of Mohammed V.

Entrance to the courtyard of the Hassan Mosque.

Hassan Tower and
Mausoleum of
Mohammed V.

Tomb of Mohammed V.

Bâb Errouah or the
Gate of the Winds in
the Almohad walls.

The magnificent 16th-century Bâb Mansour gate in Meknès.

MEKNÈS

Together with Fez, Marrakesh and Rabat, Meknès makes up the quartet of Morocco's imperial cities. It is surrounded by a triple protective wall with bastions and is made up of two clearly distinguishable areas, the modern and the old parts. In the Medina there are still several monuments dating from before the Alawid dynasty, but the present-day city grew up with the architectural style of Moulay Ismall, who reigned in the 18th century.

The name of the city is derived from that of the Meknassa, the great Berber tribe that founded Taza and Meknès. After the rule of the Almoravids, the Almohads reigned, and then the Marinids. Abu Yusuf Ya'qub al-Mansur built a new Kasbah and an enormous mosque in the second half of the 13th century, then Abu el Hassan and his son Abu Inan consolidated Meknes' urban design. After a series of vicissitudes the Alawid Sultan Moulay Ismall ennobled the city by building numerous monuments, and established close ties with the France of Louis XIV. On the death of this glorious Alawid sovereign, the city went into decline for a short time, but Sultan Sidi Mohammed Ben Abdallah was still able to provide Meknès with several mosques and to build the mausoleums of Sidi Mohammed Ben Alssa and Sidi Bou Othman. In 1755 the imperial city was affected by the earthquake that destroyed Lisbon. In 1908, Meknès played an ac-

The Bâb el-Berdaine Gate, built in the 17th century.

Entrance to the tomb of Muley Ismail.

The tomb of Muley Ismail.

Patio in the tomb of Muley Ismail. ▷

tive part in the dethronement of Sultan Moulay Abd al-Aziz. He was replaced by Moulay Afiz, in turn dethroned three years later; this gave rise to the occupation of Meknès by the French, which continued until 1956.

The Medina is of particular interest, embracing Rue Rouamazin –full of bustle and colour–, Rue Dar Smen, Place El Kdim, Bab Mansour el Aleuj, and Dar Jamaï. The visitor should also see the former imperial city with the large Place Lalla Aouda, Dar Kebira, the tomb of Moulay Ismaïl, the Garden of the Sultans, Dar el Makhzen, Bab en Nouar and Bab Merah; and the modern city with the Town Hall and the Law Courts. The markets and commercial galleries at Meknès are particularly attractive: it is possible to buy anything from magnificent Berber carpets to all kinds of artistic Moroccan craft work here.

The outstanding monuments here are the walls; the colossal Bab Mansour gate –of majestic proportions, begun shortly before the death of Moulay Ismaïl and finished around 1732 by his son Moulay Abdallah–, the largest in Meknès and one of the most famous in the whole of North Africa; the palace of Dar Jamaï, built towards the end of the 19th century, with the rooms around its beautiful garden converted since 1926 into the Museum of Moroccan Art; the artistic gate of Bâb el Khémis; the astonishingly beautiful Bâb Berdaïne gate built by Moulay Ismaïl; Moulay Ismaïl's granaries, consisting of a vast area divided into twenty-three

The majestic ruins of the Basilica and the Capitol in Volubilis.

Caracalla's triumphal arch in Volubilis.

sections; the Christians' prison, where the European captives who worked on the fortifications lived in a vast underground space; and the fine mosques –especially Bâb Berrima– appearing here and there with their characteristic architecture.

The gardens, surrounded by high walls, have a special charm in Meknès: the most outstanding are Djenan Es Souani, the Sultan's Garden and the Experimental Garden.

Another noteworthy attraction in the city is the Dar Jamaï Museum, housed in a building that belonged to the Grand Vizier Moktar, uncle of King Moulay Hassan.

Many interesting pieces are kept in this museum: paintings on wood, 18th-century pottery, finely decorated plates, beautifully embroidered cloth, manuscripts, furniture, jewels, and other objects. Pleasant excursions may be undertaken from Meknès: to Volubilis, thirty-one kilometres away, where the most important Roman ruins in Morocco stand; to Moulay Idriss, the holy city where the most important *moussem* in Morocco takes place, to which thousands of pilgrims flock; or to the luxuriant oases that lie ten kilometres to the west of Meknès.

Overall view of the Holy City of Muley Idris.

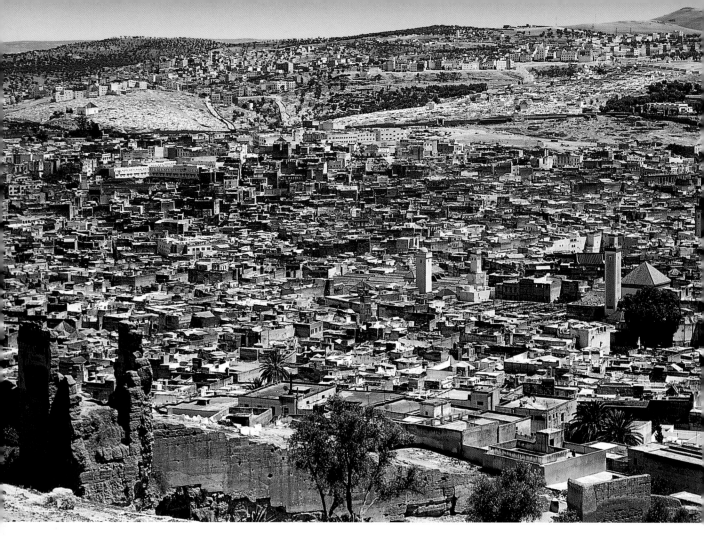

Overall view of Fez.

FEZ

Fez is the oldest of Morocco's imperial cities. Founded in 808 by Idris II, it quickly became an important trading centre and after three centuries under the Marinid dynasty it was a great city whose artistic and intellectual prestige had become known even in Europe. Fez conserves to this day the attractive appearance of a mediaeval Islamic city. The Marinid kings and those of the Alawid dynasty embellished the city with numerous monuments, many of them still excellently preserved, constituting good examples of the Hispano-Moorish style. The old city –Fez el Bali, founded by Idris II– is joined to the new one, Fez el Jedid, by the lovely gardens of Boujeloud, near Dar el Batha Museum and the palace of Dar el Beïda. The city of Fez is so extraordinarily beautiful that an Arab historian was heard to say: «Oh Fez! All the beauties of the earth are to be found in thee!».

Though the foundation of Fez is attributed to Idris II, his father, Idris I, a descendant of the Prophet, was the first to settle here, in around the year 786 or 787. After its foundation Fez welcomed many Andalusian Moslems, who helped to develop what was to be the imperial capital of Morocco. Later, in the 11th century, the Almoravids established themselves in Fez, but not without having to overcome the bitter opposition of the Béni Hammad. The Almohads succeeded the Almoravids in the 12th century, and contributed to the magnificence of the city of Fez. In the early 13th century the Marinids succeeded in eliminating the Almohads, and during the reigns of Abou er Rabi and Abou Saïd Othman in the 14th century Fez achieved extraordinary prosperity. In the 15th century Mohammed ech Cheikh, son of Yahia, the Ouattasside governor murdered by order of the last Marinid sultan, Abd el Haqq, had himself proclaimed sovereign in Fez. The Ouattasside dynasty was substituted in the 16th century by that of the Saadis, and Fez lost its status as capital of the kingdom. The city suffered several changes of fortune, but in the 18th century –during the reign of Moulay Abdallah– it became the capital once more. The Alawid dynasty contributed considerably to the greatness of the imperial capital. In the 19th century Moulay El Hassan made many changes in Fez, and it was during his reign that the Boujeloud palace and other important monuments were built. Taking advantage of the internal rivalries undermining the Sultan's authority, the French occupied Fez in 1911, and in 1912 established a protectorate which lasted until 1956.

According to tradition, the origin of the city's name derives from the fact that, when digging to lay the foundations –«in a valley situated between two high mountains covered with rich forests and watered by a thousand streams, to the right of the river of Pearls»– a large sickle (in Arabic, *fez*) weighing sixty pounds was found, and gave its name to the new imperial city. Fez was called the Mecca of the West and the Athens of Africa; in the 11th century it had a population of more than half a million inhabitants including Moors,

Boujeloud gate.

Gate to the Kasbah.

Overall night-time view of Fez. ▷

Berbers, Jews, Negroes, Turks, Christians and *renegades* (Christians converted to Islam).

The writer Edmondo d'Amicis said of Fez about a century ago that «The city stretches out in the shape of a vast figure of eight between two hills, on whose summits stand the ruins of two ancient square fortresses. Beyond the hills is a range of mountains. The river of Pearls divides the city into two: New Fez on the left bank and old Fez on the right; and old battlements with great dark towers, broken down in many parts, surround both the old and new areas. From the heights one can get a good view of the whole city: a myriad of white houses with flat roofs, with fine minarets made out of mosaic towering above, gigantic palms, masses of green, crenellated towers, and small green domes.

At first glance one can imagine the greatness of the ancient metropolis». Fez still continues to be an impressive city for its splendid, enchanting and pure evocation of mediaeval times.

There is an extraordinary wealth of monuments in this great imperial city, which still today is one of the most dynamic religious and political centres in Morocco. The outstanding sights are the medersas of Bou Inania (with its original «clock»), es Seffarîn, el Attarîn, Cherratîn, and Misbahiya; the El Qaraouiyyîn mosque, where there are sixteen aisles and 270 columns; the Andalusian's mosque with its colossal doorway; and the *zaouiya* of Moulay Idris, where the remains of the founder of Fez lie buried. But in truth the whole city is a delightful, fascinating monument, especially the old part.

The Karauina Mosque, the great mosque in Fez, holds up to 20,000 of the faithful.

There are some interesting excursions to be taken from the imperial city, among them is one to visit the large tomb where the princes of the Marinid dynasty lie buried, from whence the magnificent outline of the old city can be seen, a marvellous sight in the month of May during the famous Moroccan *son et lumière* festival. The towns of Sefrou (rich in fruit), Moulay Yacoub and Sidi Harazem (important thermal resorts) can be visited from Fez, as can Azrou, Ifrane and Kenitra. Also of interest are the slopes of Djébel Zalagh, from whence the Atlas range can be seen, Bine el ouidane dam and the Ouzoud waterfalls.

Nejarine square.

A courtyard in the Karauina Mosque.

Courtyard in the
Bouhanania medersa
(religious school).

*Front of the Royal
Palace.* ▷

Courtyard in the
Attarina medersa
(religious school).

Moroccan crafts.

*The dyers'
vats.*

Panoramic view of Casablanca.

CASABLANCA

The commercial and industrial capital of Morocco, Casablanca is most highly-populated city in the kingdom. Full of light and hospitality, Casablanca honours its name. Usually known simply as *Casa* (in Arabic Dar el Beida, «White House»), it stretches over a wide area; and its large port, situated between the promontories of Oukacha and El Hank sheltering it, has the best port installations in the whole of the African continent.

No other city of Morocco can dispute with Casablanca its status as the economic capital. The growth of this city is comparatively recent, starting at the beginning of the 20th century. After World War II its industrial development increased very rapidly; it is Morocco's foremost port and one of the busiest in all Africa: an important port of call between Europe, Africa and South America, especially Brazil and Argentina.

The greater part of Casablanca's urban outline has been carried out according to the plans drawn up by the French architects Prost and Ecochart. The city is nowadays in constant expansion, following the lines of systematic Moroccanization, which became in 1956, the year in which the country attained its independence.

The appearance of the city is distinguished architecturally by the presence of large, ultramodern buildings, contrasting markedly with other, typically Arab, edifices. The centre of Casablanca is dominated by the attractive green of the magni-

ficent Arab League Park, and its broad avenues have fine views that are comparable with those of any of the most famous thoroughfares in Paris or New York.

Apparently, the area where Casablanca now stands was inhabited by man during the Palaeolithic era. The city's origins are not known with any degree of exactitude, but it would appear that the ancient city of Anfa was located on the same site as the present-day city. Anfa played an important part in the history of Morocco at the end of the 7th century and at the beginning of the 8th century, and enjoyed particular renown in the 12th and 13th centuries. The corsairs of Anfa were attacked in 1468 by a powerful squadron commanded by Ferdinand of Portugal; and the city suffered a further attack by the Portuguese in 1515. Sixty years later the Portuguese settled in the old city, which was fortified and rebuilt and given the name Casa Blanca. Incessant attacks by neighbouring tribes and the destruction wrought by the terrible earthquake of 1755 obliged the Portuguese to leave Casablanca; in the reign of Sidi Mohammed ben Abdallah (1757-1790) it was populated by Berbers. The city was again fortified and reconstructed; at this time it was called Dar el Beida, from which the Spaniards derived the name Casablanca. In the 18th century the city became an important trading centre and about the middle of the 19th century this commercial role was augmented; in 1862 there was a regular service between Marseilles and Morocco. At the beginning of the 20th century work on the building of the mod-

The Pasha's Mahkama.

ern port was undertaken, and this constituted the basis of Casablanca's present-day economic development.

The economic importance of the city has not hindered its constantly increasing attraction for the tourist, as with the proximity to fine beaches surrounded by luxuriant vegetation and the splendid hotels, it is an ideal centre. The beaches at Pont-Blondin, Sehb Edheb, Temara, Miramar, El Har-houra, Tamaris and Azemmour (fringed with eucalyptus trees) are attractive spots for the tourist. Another visit of undoubted interest is to the famous Casablanca Aquarium, inaugurated on 3rd January 1962. The city also has splendid sports facilities for golf, tennis, riding, sailing and other activities, along with many establishments of the highest category. It is a delight to explore the city and to walk through the enchantingly picturesque old Moslem quarters.

*Patio
of the
Pasha's
Mahkama.*

Place des Nations Unies.

Place Mohammed V is the busiest part of Casablanca and its most important avenues are Avenue de l'Armée Royale (where several of the city's most important buildings are), Boulevard Mohammed al Hansali leading from Place Mohammed V to the harbour, and literally crammed with shops and boutiques, and Avenue Hassan II. Place des Nations Unies is another important centre. In the old medina, a picturesque labyrinth of small streets, a visit is recommended to the mosques of Jama el Kébir and Jama ech Chleuh; and to the Sidi el Kairouani sanctuary, built at the beginning of the 19th century in honour of Sidi Allah el Kairouani, high dignitary of Casablanca.

The Mohamadia mosque.

Twin Center, in the modern part of the city.

Marabu of Sidi Abderrahman.

Night-time view of the Hassan II mosque.

The Hassan II Mosque

After the death of his royal highness King Moham-med V in 1961, his son Hassan II, the current Moroccan monarch, considered building a mauso-leum for his father in Casablanca, where the sad event had taken place. However, the sovereign eventually decided against the idea and ordered its construction in Rabat, in order to always have his father's tomb close at hand. This decision also allows heads of states visiting the capital to medi-tate or pray before the tomb of Mohammed V should they wish to do so. Nevertheless, having reached this conclusion, Hassan II felt he was indebted to the inhabitants of Casablanca and pledged to redress this by building a great mosque there, close to the sea.

Today, those fortunate enough to see the result of this personal project of the Moroccan king are overwhelmed with admiration when contemplating the imposing profile of the finished building. Majes-tic and inspiring, the temple appears to rise out of the depths of the Atlantic ocean. Indeed, one of the principle attractions of the Mosque is that two thirds of it were constructed over water. This re-markable accomplishment being inspired by two verses of the Koran which state «The throne of God was upon the waters» and «From water have we created all life». Another fact which may give some idea of the singular nature of the Hassan II Mosque is the fact that it is the tallest religious building in the world, and the second largest in area of the Muslim world, after the Al Haramayn Acharifain Mosque in Mecca.

While the expanse of the Hassan II Mosque is vast,

One of the domes adorning the ceiling of the Oratory.

its spiritual significance for the entire Arabic and Islamic world is even greater. Situated at the extreme north-west point of what Muslims call *Dar al Islam* (the land of Islam), the Mosque proffers itself as a meeting point for the diverse civilizations which surround Morocco: the African, European, Mediterranean and Arab cultures. Thus, the sanctuary stands like a beacon, to guide an Islamic culture steeped in history on its search for greater tolerance and understanding of and from its neighbours.

The great Hassan II Mosque covers a surface area of nine hectares. Twelve thousand five hundred

View of the Oratory.

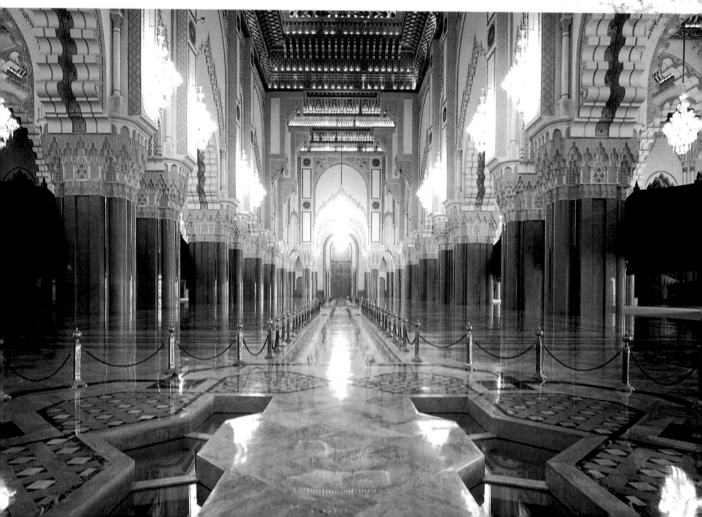

A view of the south front of the Hassan II mosque.

Two-thirds of the mosque lie on the waters of the ocean. ▷

workers, of which ten thousand were craftsmen and the rest labourers, toiled day and night in shifts in order to complete the building. To get some idea of the sheer size of the building it would be instructive to look at some of the statistics involved in its construction. Three hundred thousand cubic metres of cement were used and forty thousand tons of steel. Sixty-five thousand tons of marble and forty thousand square metres of ornamented cedar wood were utilized in its decoration. Fifty million man-hours were needed during the six years of its elaboration. King Hassan II himself took a significant role in the construction.

As the true father of the project, he personally supervised the pace of building and brought to the project many ideas and suggestions. The team of Moroccan architects and engineers, directed by Michel Pinseau, came to count on the active and enthusiastic participation of his majesty, who never hesitated in visiting the site whenever it was necessary. Of a rectangular ground plan, the Hassan II Mosque is remarkable for its size, its impressive two hundred metre high minaret which carves out the sky as it towers over Casablanca and, above all, for the extreme care which has been taken over every detail of the interior. In all, the temple remains the pearl of a religious and cultural complex which also includes a museum, a library, a Madraza (Islamic University), rooms set aside for seminars and meetings, a subterranean four lane driveway and an underground car park with capacity for one thousand, one hundred cars and forty coaches.

Walls of the old Portuguese city of El Jadida.

EL JADIDA

El Jadida, the ancient *Mazagan,* is situated in a magnificent sandy bay with rocks at either end. The remains of the old fortifications are conserved as vestiges of two and half centuries of Portuguese occupation. El Jadida used to be an important port on Morocco's Atlantic coast. At present, its outstandingly mild climate and sheltered beach make it one of the most attractive tourist centres in the kingdom.

El Jadida apparently occupies the same site as a former Phoenician trading post known as *Rusibis,* mentioned by Polybius, Ptolemy and Pliny the Elder. The Portuguese settled here in 1502 and built a fortress called el Brijia El Jadida. The city itself was also founded by the Portuguese, in 1506, and given the name Mazagan; it later became the most important Portuguese trading post on the Atlantic coast. In 1562, the Saadi Moulay Abdallah attacked the for-tress but was unable to capture it. From 1580 to 1640 El Jadida was under Spanish domination and then passed into Portuguese hands once more. A sultan of the present reigning dynasty, Sidi Mohammed ben Abdallah, succeeded in conquering the city in the year 1769; and it was rebuilt

16th-century cistern going back to the times of Portuguese rule.

around 1815 by Moulay Abd er Rahman, who gave it its present name of New El Jadida. During the period of their protectorate, the French once again called it *Mazagan* until, after the 1956 proclamation of independence, it definitively regained its Arab name of El Jadida.

It is interesting to visit the picturesque old city, that is, the part created in the period of Portuguese domination, and transformed into a Jewish quarter; this visit starts from Place Mohammed V. Among other noteworthy monuments are the old church of the Assumption –a former theatre– overlooked on the left by the pentagonal minaret of the city's main mosque, and the old Portuguese cistern, a spacious underground room which is part of the old fortress built in 1514 and a remarkable piece of military engineering. Some sequences of the film «Othello» were shot here by the director Orson Welles. The Anjo bastion, overlooking the harbour, is another interesting sight.

Minaret of El Jadida's main mosque.

Overall view of Safi.

SAFI

A former Phoenician trading post according to the geographer Ptolemy, frequented by the Romans. This town was first given the name of *Asfi* by Ibn Khaldoun. Its proximity to the Gantus mines has made Safi one of the chief phosphate processing and exporting centres in the entire world. This activity was boosted in 1965 with the opening of an industrial plant built with the technical co-operation of various European countries. Due to this important industry, the port of Safi, also well-known internationally because of its sardine fishing fleet, is the the scene of the constant comings and goings of maritime traffic.

The present site of the city of Safi was probably occupied by the ancient *Misokaras*, which Ptolomy situated between Cape Soleis and the mouth of the Fut. The city was mentioned, with the name Asfi, in the 11th century by the geographer El Bekri; and El Idrissi stated that it was a much frequented port in the 12th century. However, it was the historian Ibn Khaldoun who –in the 14th century– made the most documented references to the fortified monastery known as *Asfi*. The port remained closed to European merchants until the 15th century; about 1480 commercial contacts were initiated with Portugal. The governor of *Mogador* (Essaouira), Diego de Azambujo, and Admiral Garcia de Mello took the city in 1508 in the name of the king of Portugal, but the Portuguese abandoned the place in 1541.

Trade with Europe was intensified in the 17th century and Safi became the most important port in Morocco. Towards the end of the 18th century

View of the castle from the Kechla walls.

Sidi Mohammed built a mosque and reinforced the city's defences. During the 19th century Safi underwent a period of decline, but it was reborn in the 20th, thanks to the industrialization brought about by its canning factories and the mining of phosphates.

The most interesting monuments here include the ruins of Dar el Bahr –the castle by the sea–, built by the Portuguese at the beginning of the 16th century; Jama el Kebir –a large mosque–, the tomb of Sidi Abou Mohammed Salih –high dignitary of Safi–, the «Portuguese chapel», and the Kechla. Place de l'Independance is the city centre, and Rue du Souk the main throughfare in the old city, whose steep, narrow streets are particularly attractive.

A potters' kiln.

ESSAOUIRA

The city appears as if by magic, surrounded by water, sand and flora, white and shining, its attractive silhouette standing between the sea and the dunes of the desert. The name Essaouira comes from Al Souirah, which in Arabic means «small fortress surrounded by walls». This was the name given to the city in the 18th century. Until Morocco's proclamation of Independence, it was called *Mogador*, a name that is possibly a translation to Spanish of the Berber word Amogdul: the high dignitary of Essaouira, whose tomb is some three kilometres from the city, was called Sidi Mogdul.

The finding of remains of pottery on the islands in Essaouira bay testifies to the presence of the Phoenicians in the region from the 6th or 7th century B.C. onwards. It appears that during centuries the bay was barely frequented. However, the main island was once again populated at the end of the 1st century AD, this time on a permanent basis.

Essaouira wall.

The city of Essaouira itself, sited on a promontory on *terra firma,* was apparently founded in the 18th century. Earlier, at the beginning of the 16th century, the Portuguese had built a fortress which was restored by Moulay Abd el Malek in 1628. The city was in fact founded by Sidi Mohammed Ben Abdallah, a member of the still reigning Alawid dynasty.

Essaouira, surrounded by high walls, is divided by means of interior walls into three clearly differentiated urban areas: the Medina, the Mellah and the Kasbah. There are many lovely gardens within the city, forming areas of delicious coolness. The outstanding monuments here are the Porte de la Marine with the figure 1769 (the date of its construction) marked on the pediment, the Sqala in the harbour –an old battery whose cannons were made in Spain–, the Sqala in the Kasbah –an impressive platform some two hundred metres long– and the sanctuary of Moulay Abd el Kader el Jilali.

There is a splendid beach at Essaouira, with fine sand, where the climate is always mild because it is sheltered by the island in the bay.

Marine Gate.

Night-time view of Jemaa El-Fna Square.

MARRAKESH

This is one of Morocco's imperial cities and the second oldest in the country. Known as «the pearl of the south», Marrakesh was founded by the Almoravids in the late 11th century. The most attractive place in the southern part of the country between the Atlas and the Sahara, it is an impressive sight to see this city from a distance surrounded by its palm groves, in the middle of the blazing hot plain of Haouz; in winter and in spring the peaks of nearby Mount Atlas are covered with snow.

It seems that the Berber Abou Bekr, the brave chief of an Almoravid tribe, was the founder of the city. His nephew Youssef ben Tachfin built a mosque and established himself in Marrakesh while Abou Bekr was in the Sahara fighting a group of rebels. Afterwards, when Abou Bekr came back, Youssef Ben Tachfin crossed the strait of Gibraltar and defeated the troops of Alphonso VI, enriching Marrakesh with his conquests and war trophies. The city developed considerably and became the most important trading centre in Morocco. In the 12th century, Abd el Mumin founded the Almohad dynasty. Marrakesh lived a period of great splendour under the Marinids, whose most famous Sultan was Ahmed el Mansour. On his death the city went through a period of decline. But Marrakesh regained its lost splendour, during the reign of the Alawid dynasty. Towards the end of the 19th cen-

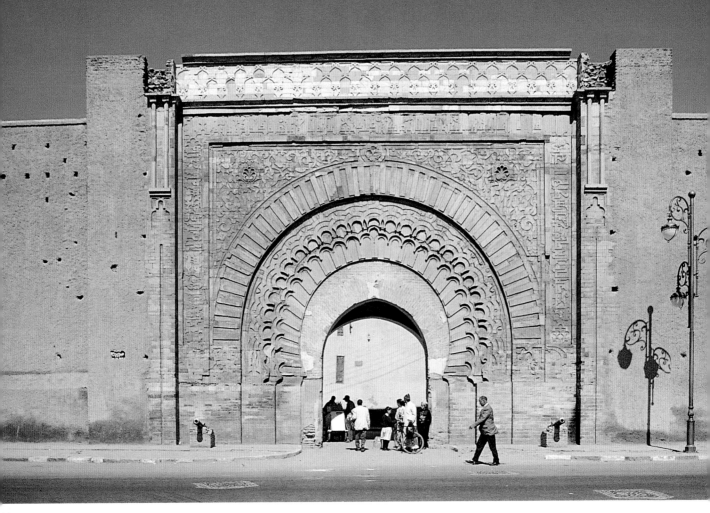

Bâb Aguenaou, built in the 12th century.

La Koutoubia Mosque, or «Mosque of the Booksellers».

El-Badi Palace.

The mosque where the Saadis' tombs are found.

tury, Sultan Moulay Hassan enlarged the city, as did his son Moulay Abdal-Aziz; many of the buildings in it are owed to them.

Marrakesh is the great city of the Berbers. It has successfully preserved the pure mediaeval structure of the period of its foundation, the greater part of its architectural wealth dating from the period of the Almohads and the Saadis. The Almohads built the Koutoubia mosque, with its famous minaret, the Ben Youssef medersa (Moslem religious school) with its fine mosaic work, marble and valuable wood carvings; but it was the Saadis who had the honour of constructing the fascinating, impressive tombs containing the remains of the monarchs of this dynasty. other monuments of importance in

Marrakesh include the Mouassîn and «Chrob ou Chouf» («drink and admire») fountains, the Bâb Agnaou gate –in pure Almohad style– and the 19th-century Bahia palace, with its splendid gardens.

The Dar Si Saïd Museum is particularly important: situated in a palace built in 1900, which in 1914 became the residence of the chiefs of the Marrakesh region. After being restored in 1932 it was converted into the Museum of Moroccan Art, where valuable Berber jewellery is on show, together with a collection of velvet caftans embroidered with golden thread, ceramics, tapestries, carpets, tooled leather objects, weapons from many different places and mosaics.

Marrakesh, with its colourful, dynamic markets and

The Saadis' tombs.

The great courtyard in the Bahia Palace.

extraordinary wealth of handicrafts, is one of the most attractive cities in the whole of Morocco. It can be said that it is a city that has kept its heritage of folklore in all its fascinatingly original richness. The Marrakesh Festival is usually celebrated in the month of May; the highest point of picturesque splendour is the daily folklore celebration centred on Place Jemaa el Fna, the veritable heart of the city.

The most important avenues in the city are the Avenue Mohammed V, Avenue Hassan II, Avenue El Menara, Avenue de France, Avenue du Président Kennedy, Avenue des Nations Unies, Boulevard de Safi and Rue El Irak.

Interior of the Bahia Palace.

*Bahia
Palace.*

Menara Park.

Marrakesh: Ben Yusef
Medersa (religious
school), an architectural
masterpiece.

Dyers' quarter.
Young Moroccan girls dressed in traditional costume.

Place Jemaa el Fna, already mentioned, is the nerve-centre of Marrakesh and is near the Bahia Palace, the Royal Palace, the tombs of the Sultans of the Saadi dynasty, the Koutoubia and Bâb Doukkala mosques and the medersa of Ben Youssef.
There are many interesting excursions to be taken from Marrakesh, including the palm groves itinerary, with about 150,000 trees; and to Amizmiz, crossing the Haouz plain dominated by the colossal Atlas mountains, visiting wonderful spots such as the kasbah at Tamesloht or the golden town of Oumnast; the ouzoud waterfalls; the natural bridge at Imin'Ifri; or the lovely lake at Aït Aadel.

Water bearers.

Ouzoud waterfall, where the river crashes down a 100-metre chasm of green, some 150 km northwest of Marrakech.

Taurirt Kasbah.

OUARZAZATE

This town was founded in 1928 and has a comfortable tourist hotel with attractive city views, pure Berber-style castles and the vast sun-drenched plain surrounding it. Ouarzazate is encircled by picturesque villages which still preserve their pure Moroccan-style folklore.

Carpet-weaving.

View of the Taroudannt walls.

TAROUDANNT

This charming city was once the capital of the Sous region –a large plain bathed in sunlight gilding the hillsides and enriching the earth–. Taroudannt is famous for its unusual, artistic, craft work. The carved stones, Berber jewels and old weapons are much appreciated.

Taroudannt has a long history. At the beginning of the 11th century the city was the capital of a Shiah principality, established with the help of the Fatimids of Ifrikuiya. In 1056 it fell into the hands of the Almoravids but gained its independence during the Almohad period, under the leadership of the Yedder family. After being destroyed in the 14th century, the city's fortifications were rebuilt and it became the metropolitan city of Sous. In the 16th century, after regaining its independence, Taroudannt enjoyed a period of splendour and was an important centre for trade with the Sudan. Later, in the time of Mohammed Ibn Abd er Rahman, the city became the centre of resistance against the Portuguese who had settled in Agadir. After the Portuguese fortress of Cap Rhir was taken, Taroudannt lost its status as the Saadi capital, until Mohammed ech Cheikh conquered Marrakesh. Because of the support it had lent to the cause of Ahmed Ibn Mahrez in the 17th century, the Alawid sultan Moulay Ismaïl conquered Taroudannt in 1687. Towards the end of the 19th

Mosque, Taroudannt.

century it became a centre of intrigue against the central authority until 1913.

Its narrow winding streets and narrow Place d'Assarag flanked by picturesque markets, lend the city of Taoroudannt an enchanting air for the tourist. The city has a distinctive appearance, surrounded by crenellated walls, gardens, olive trees and palms.

There are some good hotels here; and the craftsmen's quarter of the city is well worth a visit. There are interesting excursions from here by road to Freija, Tiout –where there is a fine panoramic view of the Sous valley– and to Amagour, on the spurs of the Anti-Atlas.

Craft market.

Trafaoute: a typical hilltop village.

Panoramic view of Trafaoute.

TAFRAOUTE

The scenery here is of exceptional beauty. An enormous elemental mass of rounded red rocks that seem to keep their balance by means of some strange, complicated mechanism, it looks like a fantastic kasbah of ochre-red walls surmounted by white battlements contrasting with the green tones of the vegetation: an original, harmonious picture. Mount Tafraoute sometimes takes on amethyst tones and the summits are as if crowned with bold tones that dazzle the visitor.

This little mountain is situated in the west of the Anti-Atlas, between Agadir and Tiznit. The excursion to Tafraoute is one of the most delightful ones that can be undertaken in the south of Morocco. There is an excellent hotel belonging to the Diafa chain at the foot of the mountain, with splendid facilities laid on expressly for tourists.

The Dra Valley is characterised by its palm trees,
innumerable fortresses and tiny Berber villages.

Panoramic view of the Dra Valley.

Panoramic view of the Dades Valley.

The majestic kasbah of Skoura in the Dades Valley

Overall view of Tineghir.

TINEGHIR

The oasis of Tineghir, famous for its palm trees and many kasbahs, is one of the largest and loveliest in Morocco. It abounds in luxuriant vegetation and is situated close to the Todgha. The town is a former military post situated on the route from Ouarzazate to Ksar es Souk, and is terraced around a hill on top of which stands the old castle of the Glaoui (an old pasha in Morocco) as well as the Grand Hôtel Sagro.

One of Tineghir's outstanding tourist attractions –apart from the delightful excursions that can be taken from the oasis– is the quality of the Berber jewellery in silver and other metals made in the locality.

The visitor can enjoy broad, beautiful panoramas from the terraces of Glaoui palace and the Grand Hôtel Sagro. A trip through the palm groves towards Tagoumast is certainly worthwhile, returning by the P32 road from Ksar es Souk; the Todgha gorges make another good excursion.

The Todra Gorge, with its 300-metre high rock walls.

One of the many fortified old villages in the Ziz Valley.

Kasbah in the holy city of Rissani.

In the city of Imilchil, the traditional «mussem» is celebrated each September. Nomad tribes from all over the region gather to strengthen family ties and arrange marriages between families.

Aerial view of Agadir beach.

AGADIR

An important sea resort, Agadir is a city of considerable attraction for the tourist as, apart from the privilege of its ideal climate, it has a magnificent beach, the longest in all Morocco. Agadir is at the foot of an impressive cliff topped by an imposing 16th-century citadel which was restored in the 18th century, overlooking the picturesque Funti quarter, part of the modern city, and the harbour. In spite of having been partly destroyed by a terrible earthquake in 1960, this fine Moroccan city has regained its dynamism and former elegance.

Agadir is of very ancient origins and many authors have identified it with the ancient port of *Russadir* mentioned by Polybius. Apparently the Carthaginian admiral Hannon visited *Russadir.* in 1505 the Portuguese João Lopes de Sequeira built a small fort known as Santa Cruz de Cap Rhir close to what is now Agadir, at Aït Funti. Eight years later this fort was sold to the king of Portugal.

From 1531 onwards Mohammed ech Cheikh established a military base at Tamragh, some twelve kilometres away, which fell into Moroccan hands on 12th March 1541 after several previous attacks. Agadir played an important part as a commercial centre in the 17th century, with Denmark gaining the monopoly of its trade in 1751. Sultan Sidi Mohammed ben Abdallah halted Agadir's commercial activities so as to stimulate the develop-

Two views of Agadir.

Fishing port.

ment of trade at Essaouira. Agadir underwent a period of decline throughout the 19th century, but in the 20th it once more became a flourishing city. The most attractive feature of Agadir is its Kasbah, a veritable eyrie perched 236 metres above sea level: built in the year 1540 by Mohammed ech Cheikh as a starting point from which to launch his offensive against the Portuguese fortress, and restored in 1752, this is a fine vantage point with a magnificent view of the sea.

The modern city, with its urban development and level districts separated by vast green spaces, is pleasant to the eye as it has been built with a coherent, rational architectural policy in mind.

The most important monuments in Agadir are the main mosque, the law court, the Town Hall, and the Post Office building.

Its main shopping streets either branch out from Avenue Hassan II or are situated nearby: they are Avenue des Forces Armées Royales and Boulevard Mohammed V. The lovely Ibn Zidoun gardens are also certainly worth visiting.

On the outskirts of the city, from Cap Rhir onwards, there are many beaches and coves which make Agadir a first-rate tourist centre.

Many interesting excursions can be taken from the city to Tafraoute and to the lovely Saharan palm groves at Bani.

TIZNIT

This is a picturesque town located some 100 kilometres from Agadir, and famous for its craft work. The worked Berber silver jewellery and decoratively encrusted weapons are the typical products of Tiznit and constitute a great tourist attraction.

Tiznit was founded in 1882, by Moulay el Hassan during a military expedition. The city then became an important trading centre. In 1919, the city was occupied by the French, who stayed until 1956, when Morocco was proclaimed independent.

Tiznit is an unusually attractive place, with a mosque surrounded by palm trees with a minaret in Sudanese style, the Medina and Jewish quarter, and its winding streets where there are many jewellers' shops.

Interesting excursions can be made from Tiznit, to the Anti-Atlas and Foum el Hassan, Akka, Tata and Foum Zguid, localities with luxuriant palm trees close to the immense Sahara desert. A trip to Goulimine is also interesting: the market here is a particularly attractive spot for the Saharan camel-drivers, being the first of a series of oases in the foothills of the Bani mountains.

To get a good idea of Tiznit's popular characteristics it is necessary to visit the great mosque and to stroll in a leisurely fashion along the itinerary from Bâb Targua to Bâb el Khemis, wandering in the intricate paths and admiring the landscape, dotted everywhere with palm trees.

Great Mosque, Tiznit.

Entrance to Goulimine and the gate to the desert.

The zoco in Goulimine attracts tribespeople from the surrounding area.

Erg Chebbi dunes, Erfoud.

The fishing village of Tarfaya.

Dunes of the Sahara: caravan.

Laâyoune. ▷

THE SAHARAN PROVINCES

Lying the southernmost part of Morocco, flanked by the Atlantic Ocean on the one side and Mauritania on the other, the Saharan provinces cover an area around 1,000 kilometres long by a width varying between 280 and 500 kilometres. The Saharan landscape is characterised by the capricious forms of dunes running through which it is not unusual to find old paths used long ago by the desert caravans, as well as tiny streams which rarely reach the nearby sea. Since 1976, when Spain granted Morocco sovereignty over the region, the population of the Saharan provinces has grown steadily, due to a large entent to the process of modernisation undertaken since. Laâyoune, the largest centre of population, combines the legacy of its past with more recent architectural and works and town planning developments sponsored by the Moroccan authorities. The construction of new urban zones, gradually occupied by nomadic tribespeople from the surrounding area, does not, however, blot out the mark left by the Spanish in the form of various old administrative buildings and a church.

Other inhabited areas of outstanding interest include the holy city of Smara, with the ruins of an old fortress and the Great Mosque, and the fishing village of Ad Dakhla, founded by the Spanish with the name Villa Cisneros.

Overall view of the city of Tangier.

TANGIER

From its ideal position on a strategic amphitheatre of hills, this attractive white city stands opposite the straits of Gibraltar, its excellent port links Europe and Africa by sea. Tangier is a city with a distinct personality, the past and the present mingling harmoniously in its appearance: typically Moroccan charm juxtaposed with the functional design of the large, ultra-modern buildings.

The origins of ancient *Tingis* are shrouded in legend; according to Hellenic mythology, the city of Tangier was founded by the famous king Antheus. During the period of Roman domination it became the capital of the province of *Mauretania Tingitana*.

In 429 the city was occupied by the Vandals, led by Genseric. Later it became a dependency of the Byzantine Empire. It was from Tangier that the ships under Tarik set sail in 711 to begin the conquest of Spain. After the passage of the Almoravids and the Almohads, the city suffered different adventures; it was conquered by the Portuguese in 1471 and reconquered by Moulay Ismaïl at the end of the 17th century.

After having enjoyed a special status for many years, as a consequence of the Algeciras Conference in 1906, Tangier was definitively incorporated into the kingdom of Morocco when the latter became independent in 1956. The city has an unusually attractive atmosphere: the evocative Great

Socco and Small Socco (markets), the gardens of the Sultan, with the dominating presence of the Great Mosque, the mysterious, white, zigzagging structure of the Kasbah with the old palace founded by Moulay Ismaïl containing the Moroccan Art Museum and the Archaeological Museum, the Dar ech Cherâ (Moslem law courts) and Bab el Assa make up a varied scene full of authentic Arab vitality, connected via Rue d'Italie and Rue Ben Raisoul with the dynamic modern city with its fine avenues, restaurants, magnificent sports facilities and lovely beach.

Tangier is an eminently touristic city, with visitors from every part of the world coming all the year round. Everything is welcoming in Tangier, beginning with the pleasant nature of its inhabitants. The climate is very agreeable and the hotels, extremely comfortable.

Various interesting excursions can be undertaken from the city: the Cap Spartel itinerary, where there are magnificent views of the sea and the mountains; the grottoes of Hercules; *Cotta,* a former Punic and Roman trading post; and Cap Malabata –attractive places such as these follow one upon another along the road skirting the bay– and the city of Asilah.

Avenue d'Espagne with, in the background, the Medina.

Place 9 Avril and the
Great Zoco.

The minaret of the
Kasbah mosque. ▷

Small Zoco.

Two views of the
Kasbah walls.

Cave of Hercules,
where prehistoric
remains have been
found.

Kasbah and El-Homar gates in the nearby city of Asilah.

A street in the «white city» of Asilah.

Sidi Mansur wall in Asilah.

AL HOCEIMA

This city was founded in 1926 by the Spaniards, who gave it the name of Villa Sanjurjo. Al Hoceima is destined to become an important tourist centre on the Mediterranean coast of Morocco. There is a port with deep water and rugged cliffs overlooking the magnificent bay of Alhucemas.

The beautiful white buildings of Al Hoceima stretch from the hills to the sea shore. The city streets are picturesquely bustling, dominated by Avenue Mohammed V, Place du Rif and Place Hassan II.

Al Hoceima is an important thermal resort and has an ultra modern hotel. Since 1965 a series of small bungalows have been built along the hillsides.

The bay is protected by three islets; on one of them, the *Peñón de Alhucemas,* stands the old Spanish fortress, a fantastic sight when illuminated at night.

The waters of the bay are ideal for sailing and underwater fishing.

Al Hoceima is situated at the fork of the roads to Tétouan and Nador.

View of Al Hoceima.

Overall view of Tétouan.

TÉTOUAN

An important city on the hill of Dersa, only sixty kilometres from Tangier, Tétouan is surrounded by lovely countryside with many gardens watered by the river Martil. This is one of the most genuinely Arab cities in the Mediterranean area of Morocco. Founded at the beginning of the 14th century by the Marinid sultan Abu Thabit, Tétouan is situated near the ancients' *Tamuda*. The city soon became highly prosperous, but Henry III of Castile destroyed it in 1399, killing half its inhabitants and deporting the rest to Europe. After being repopulated at the beginning of the 16th century, it became an active trading centre. After several changes of fortune, Tétouan enjoyed a period of splendour in the 18th century, during the reign of Moulay Ismaïl. The city was occupied by the Spaniards in the middle of the last century; and became definitively incorporated into the kingdom of Morocco in 1956.

Tétouan displays attractive city walls, many mosques (Sidi es Saldi is the most outstanding), picturesque streets with delightful archways over them, Bâb er Remous gate (from which there is a fine panoramic view of the valley of the river Martil), the royal palace, and the white houses of the city. The nearby Roman ruins at Tamuda are also of interest.

Tétouan furthermore offers the splendid beach of the river Martil, some twenty-five kilometres long.

Rue de la Medina.

There are two important museums in Tetouan: the Archaeological Museum (with interesting Roman pieces, fragments of Iberian and Greco-Punic pottery, jewels, coins and the two large mosaics discovered at Lixus, depicting the Three Graces and an infant Bacchus) and the Moroccan Folklore and Art Museum.

There are some interesting excursions from here, to El Ksar es Séghir (where the Arabs going to wage the holy war in Spain used to embark; there is an old Portuguese citadel), to Zinat, where Raissouni was born, and to Tangier.

Rue Yamaa El Kebir

Entry to Rue Zavia Jarrak. ▷

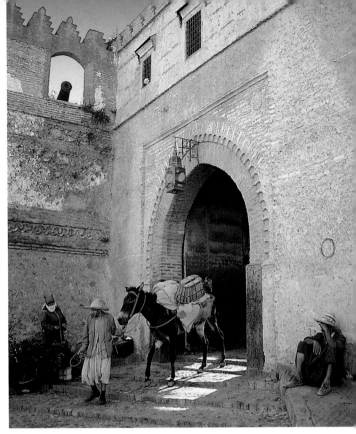

Queen's Gate.

Mosque and Place Hassan II.

Overall view of Chéchaouen, and a view of one of its streets.

CHÉCHAOUEN

A charming little city at 610 metres above sea level,
Chéchaouen is defended by imposing rocks and is
extremely picturesque in appearance. Its white buildings and many green spaces and fountains make it a
real garden city. Founded in the late 15th century by
Moulay Ben Rachid, it still preserves from its past
glory a fortress with a mediaeval turret. The main
points of interest are the Medina, with its one-storey
white washed houses; Uta el-Hammam square be-
side the fortress walls; and the Great Mosque, which
dates to the 15th century. There are also half a dozen
mosques and many sanctuaries. Situated as it is in
the middle of the Rif mountains, Chéchaouen is an
attractive place for tourists, like a miracle of civiliza-
tion amid the stern Rif scenery. There is an interesting
museum and an excellent hotel in Chéchaouen.
This is a city with a great future in tourism: an ideal
starting point for excursions in the Rif mountains that
line the Mediterranean seaboard from the strait of
Gibraltar to the mouth of the Moulouya on the
Morocco-Algeria frontier.

INDEX

ESCUDO DE ORO, S.A. COLLECTIONS

ALL SPAIN

1 MADRID
2 BARCELONA
3 SEVILLE
4 MAJORCA
5 THE COSTA BRAVA
8 CORDOBA
9 GRANADA
10 VALENCIA
11 TOLEDO
12 SANTIAGO
13 IBIZA and Formentera
14 CADIZ and provincia
15 MONTSERRAT
17 TENERIFE
20 BURGOS
21 ALICANTE
24 SEGOVIA
25 SARAGOSSA
26 SALAMANCA
27 AVILA
28 MINORCA
29 SAN SEBASTIAN and Guipúzcoa
30 ASTURIAS
31 LA CORUNNA and the Rías Altas
32 TARRAGONA
40 CUENCA
41 LEON
42 PONTEVEDRA, VIGO and Rías Bajas
43 RONDA
46 SIGUENZA
47 ANDALUSIA
52 EXTREMADURA
54 MORELLA
58 VALLDEMOSSA

GUIDES

1 MADRID
2 BARCELONA
3 LA RIOJA
4 MAJORCA
6 SANTIAGO DE COMPOSTELA
7 SEVILLA
8 ANDALUCIA
9 GRAN CANARIA
12 GALICIA
13 CORDOBA
14 COSTA BLANCA
15 GRANADA
22 SEGOVIA
25 AVILA
26 HUESCA
28 TOLEDO
30 SANTANDER

---

4 LONDON

---

1 LA HABANA VIEJA
2 EL CAPITOLIO (CUBA)

ALL EUROPE

1 ANDORRA
2 LISBON
3 LONDON
4 BRUGES
6 MONACO
7 VIENNA
11 VERDUN
12 THE TOWER OF LONDON
13 ANTWERP
14 WESTMINSTER ABBEY
15 THE SPANISH RIDING
   SCHOOL IN VIENNA
17 WINDSOR CASTLE
18 LA CÔTE D'OPAL
19 COTE D'AZUR
22 BRUSSELS
23 SCHÖNBRUNN PALACE
25 CYPRUS
26 HOFBURG PALACE
27 ALSACE
28 RHODES
30 CORFU
31 MALTA
32 PERPIGNAN
33 STRASBOURG
34 MADEIRA + PORTO SANTO
35 CERDAGNE - CAPCIR
36 BERLIN
42 CONFLENT-CANIGOU

TOURISM

1 COSTA DEL SOL
2 COSTA BRAVA
3 ANDORRA
4 ANTEQUERA
6 MENORCA
8 MALLORCA
9 TENERIFE
14 LA ALPUJARRA
15 LA AXARQUIA
16 PARQUE ARDALES AND EL CHORRO
17 NERJA
18 GAUDI
19 BARCELONA
21 MARBELLA
23 LA MANGA DEL MAR MENOR
25 CATEDRAL DE LEON
26 MONTSERRAT
34 RONDA
35 IBIZA-FORMENTERA
37 GIRONA
38 CADIZ
39 ALMERIA
40 SAGRADA FAMILIA
42 FATIMA
43 LANZAROTE
44 MEZQUITA HASSAN II
45 JEREZ DE LA FRONTERA
46 PALS
47 FUENGIROLA
48 SANTILLANA DEL MAR
49 LA ALHAMBRA Y EL GENERALIFE
51 MONACO-MONTECARLO

ALL AMERICA

1 PUERTO RICO
2 SANTO DOMINGO
3 QUEBEC
4 COSTA RICA
5 CARACAS
6 LA HABANA

---

1 CUZCO
2 AREQUIPA
3 LIMA
4 MACHU PICCHU

ALL AFRICA

1 MOROCCO
3 TUNISIA

ART IN SPAIN

1 PALAU DE LA MUSICA CATALANA
2 GAUDI
3 PRADO MUSEUM I
   (Spanish Painting)
4 PRADO MUSEUM I
   (Foreing Painting)
5 MONASTERY OF GUADALUPE
7 THE FINE ARTS MUSUEM OF SEVILLE
10 THE CATHEDRAL OF GIRONA
11 GRAN TEATRO DEL LICEO
   (Great Opera House
14 PICASSO
15 ROYAL PALACE OF SEVILLE
19 THE ALHAMBRA AND THE GENERALIFE
21 ROYAL ESTATE OF ARANJUEZ
22 ROYAL ESTATE OF EL PARDO
24 ROYAL PALACE OF SAN ILDEFONSO
26 OUR LADY OF THE PILLAR OF
   SARAGOSSA
27 TEMPLE DE LA SAGRADA FAMILIA
28 POBLET ABTEI
29 THE CATHEDRAL OF SEVILLE
30 THE CATHEDRAL DE MAJORCA
32 MEZQUITA DE CORDOBA
33 GOYA
34 THE CATHEDRAL OF BARCELONA
35 CASA - MUSEU CASTELL GALA-DALI
   PUBOL
36 THE CATHEDRAL OF SIGUENZA
37 SANTA MARIA LA REAL DE NAJERA
38 CASA - MUSEU SALVADOR DALI
   PORT LLIGAT

MONOGRAPHS (S)

5 SOLAR ENERGY IN THE CERDAGNE
10 MORELLA
20 CAPILLA REAL DE GRANADA
31 CORDILLERAS DE PUERTO RICO
38 GIBRALTAR
50 BRUGES
68 MONASTERIO DE PIEDRA
70 TORREVIEJA
74 VALLDEMOSSA
75 ANTWERP
84 CATHEDRAL OF MAJORCA
85 CATHEDRAL OF BARCELONA
86 VALL D'UXO

MONOGRAPHS (L)

5 PUERTO RICO
6 THE OLD SAN JUAN
9 THE CITY OF BRUGES
19 MURALLAS DE SAN JUAN

MAPS

1 MADRID
2 BARCELONA
6 LONDON
8 ALICANTE
20 PANAMA
31 SEVILLE
33 BRUGES
36 SEGOVIA
37 CORDOBA
38 CADIZ
40 PALMA OF MAJORCA
45 JEREZ DE LA FRONTERA
47 AVILA
48 ANDORRA
50 SALAMANCA
52 LEON
53 BURGOS
58 IBIZA
78 GRANADA
80 MONACO
93 MENORCA
94 LA MANGA DEL MAR MENOR
96 COSTA BRAVA
97 LLORET DE MAR
98 SANTANDER

EDITORIAL ESCUDO DE ORO, S.A.
I.S.B.N. 84-378-0917-7
Printed by FISA - Escudo de Oro, S.A.
Palaudarias, 26 - 08004 Barcelona
Dep. Legal B. 29874-1999

Protegemos el bosque, papel procedente de cultivos forestales controlados
Wir schützen den Wald. Papier aus kontrollierten Forsten.
We protect our forests. The paper used comes from controlled forestry plantations
Nous sauvegardons la forêt: papier provenant de cultures forestières controlées

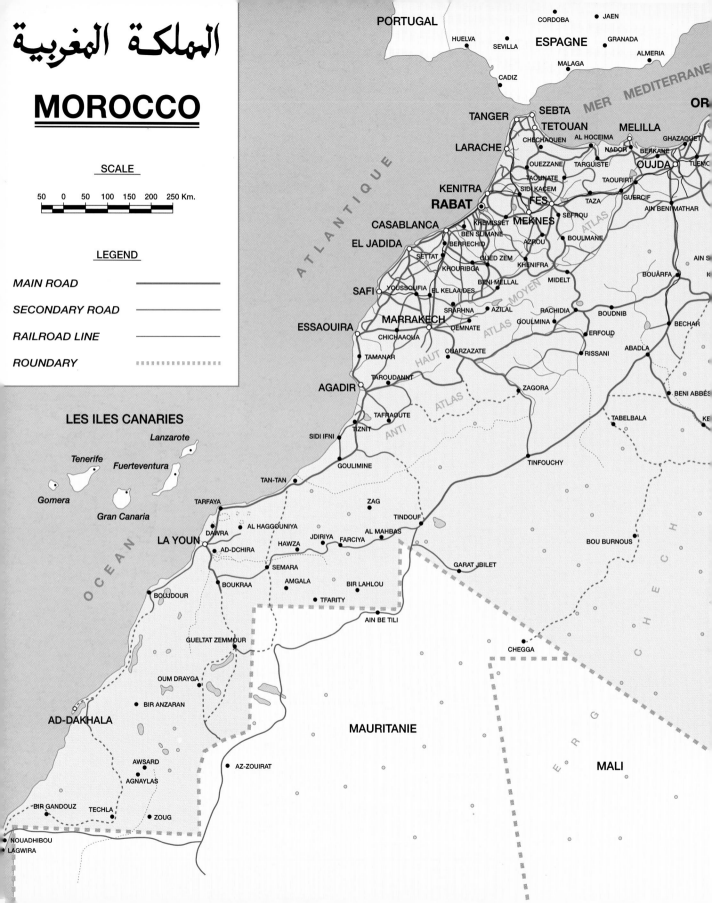